Creating a Solo Writer's Retreat

Actualizing Undisturbed Time & Space to Write Within Our Busy Lives

Kermie Wohlenhaus

ISBN: 9798735317234

Creating a Solo Writer's Retreat

Kermie Wohlenhaus

"If you've ever needed time alone to focus on your writing this is the book for you. Kermie Wohlenhaus' extensive research and real-life examples will answer all your questions even before you know what they are."

- Penelope Starr, author of *The Radical Act of Community Storytelling*

"A little Gem of a book......for every writer's library."

- Jeanne Bjorn, author of *Attuned: Reclaiming our Emotional Intelligence*

Creating a Solo Writer's Retreat

Kermie Wohlenhaus

Dedicated to all who write . . .

and those who want to

Table of Contents

Kermie Wohlenhaus

Introduction

The dog needs walked, the phone needs answered, the kids need attention, the spouse is talking, someone is at the door – it goes on and on, and on. When do we ever have time to write? Writing at home is full of distractions that can derail us from our writing-track goals. Writing gets shoved to the bottom of the never-ending "To Do" list. We vow to do better tomorrow – to follow our writing dreams.

But, what happens? Tomorrow's intentions are again diverted and the time and energy we want to spend writing is eaten up with tasks, engagements, and responsibilities. We write snippets here and there as we catch precious moments, in the bathroom, on the porch, at the kitchen table. Even there, people are wanting in, stopping by, or asking questions.

Living alone seems to be the answer, but again, writing can easily be interrupted, sidetracked, or sabotaged. The telephone, social media, TV, friends, weddings, parties, funerals, shopping, family, and errands – all hungry for our attention. How can we ever create more space in our busy lives to have extended, undisturbed time to write? We have to – it is essential to our well-being and lives.

When we writers don't write, we tilt a bit off center. Something is deeply wrong within our souls. We become quick to anger, uncomfortable, and distracted. Our muse nags us throughout the day and seeps into the night, never letting up. Write, write, write. We want to, but time slips away like water through our fingers.

I would fantasize about going to a cozy mountain cabin and getting snowed in, suddenly gifted with all the time in the world to write. Or I'd dream of being on a secluded island, writing on the deck of a beach house over-looking the ocean. I could almost feel the sea breeze in my hair as I worked on my latest project. Even though these writing retreats sounded fabulous, the reality is they take a lot of planning and money. I could only gift myself one of these writing retreats for a week or two, once or twice a year. It wasn't enough. I had to create solo writer's retreats, as many and as cheaply, and as soon as possible. The good news is, going away to write is not only a reality for those with wealth and fame; it is available to all of us who want and need it.

I have found a simple solution to avoid constant interferences and find private time and space to write. It is to create a solo writer's retreat, and the first step is simply *getting out of the house*. It can be as easy as discovering places to write that are far enough away that we are not visibly accessible, but reachable in case of an emergency. We can create extended writing opportunities that can fit neatly within our hectic schedules.

These writing get-a-ways are only a matter of looking for and taking the action to gift ourselves a few hours or days alone to write. Solo writing retreats enable us to be immensely productive within our present financial and worldly obligations – and we can still have a vibrant home life.

The goal of this book is to give you practical suggestions on how to manifest small and large solo writing retreats. They can be simple or extravagant, expensive or free, it is all up to you.

Other writers began to ask me how I could go on so many writing retreats throughout the year. I was asked to give presentations and workshops to writers on how to create these solo writing retreats. As I shared what I had learned and listened to other writers, material for a book began to take shape. This is that book.

Included within these pages are tips and ideas to assist you to create many productive solo writing retreats in your own life. If you want to write more, to have private and prolific writing time, this is the book for you. I will guide you through the steps I took. The first step was vital, and it all started with changing a core belief.

The Biggest Barrier to a Writing Retreat

Before my first solo writer's retreat, I discovered my biggest barrier – my negative thinking was sabotaging my positive action. I would sigh and tell myself that when I had more money, or more time, or when I could quit my job, retire, or when the family responsibilities lessened, *then* I would go on a writing retreat. As you know, that never happened, for there was always something to keep me from realizing this vision.

One day, I made the true connection – the *something* keeping me from actualizing this dream was *ME*. My *thoughts* kept me from manifesting this much-needed extended writing time. I *believed* what I was telling myself. I had no time, not enough money, and too many responsibilities to actually come up with creative solutions that worked for me. I had to stop *believing* there wasn't enough. The reality I wanted to create was – there was *more* than enough time and space to write. I just had to find a way to access that energy and begin to turn those negative thoughts and beliefs around. I was tired of that sad old story. I wanted a happier one.

I had to instead affirm, "Yes, I *am* going to have a writing retreat, many in fact, and I *am* creating them for myself *now*!" Not sometime when I would have a different life and circumstances. I had to ask myself, "How can I go on a writer's retreat in the very near future?" This shift to the right direction in my thinking has changed my writing life.

Taking Action

After that, I took action to see what was already being done. I searched the internet for the various paid or sponsored writer's and poetry retreats, colonies, and residencies. These websites had photos and descriptions of enticing secluded locations throughout the country and world.

There was usually a submission process for acceptance. Then after confirmation there was air flights to configure, scheduling, the arranging of transportation to and from, and so forth. For those who have trouble with initiating writing, keeping on a writing track, or needing a strict schedule, this type of regimented writing retreat may be ideal. Know yourself and what works for you.

These writer's retreats are grand and can be wildly productive, with opportunities to meet and glean skills from other writers. Please take advantage of any and all opportunities –

the more writing retreats, the better. Avail yourself to all paths that motivate and inspire. But thinking of them and the details involved often got me stuck again and became writing time eaters just to make it all happen.

I knew of some writer's groups who went on writing retreats together. This took a massive amount of energy coordinating schedules, securing accommodations, seeking transportation options, and working with each person's sensitivities, personalities, and expectations. These can also be beneficial, as you know your group, but again, this sort of retreat usually happens only once or twice a year. With solo retreats, we only have to schedule with ourselves and get out the door. So much easier and quicker!

As I was exploring these group or paid options, my immediate need for a writer's retreat seemed to grow in intensity daily. I finally had to find a way to put private writing retreats into my life as soon as possible. I could not wait months or until next year. It had to be now!

What I Needed

I began to seriously brainstorm and list what I really needed in the way of a writing retreat. Being honest with myself was vital in this process. What would help me be a productive writer? After much thought, I came up with my ideal writer's retreat to enhance my writing life while supporting my personal idiosyncrasies.

This is what I came up with:

I needed a writer's retreat to occur more often than my two-week vacation once a year. I needed time to write at least daily/weekly/monthly. I also wanted to keep my part-time job and not constantly take time off of work.

I wanted my writing retreats to be within driving distance so I could use my own car. Studying Google Maps gave me information about towns and locations that were within a one-to-three-hour drive from my home. I didn't want to spend my valuable writing time on long drives.

My finances dictated spending within a certain amount. I began setting aside money daily for this purpose – saving pocket change and stowing one and five-dollar bills in an envelope. I'd forgo the extra expense of something that I wanted and stuck with only those purchases I needed, for the want of a writing retreat was much more compelling than that extra lip balm, event ticket, or dessert. I began to carry hard candy and protein bars to satisfy my snack need to avoid buying anything snacky or a meal while I was out.

I had to find affordable accommodations. I began to ask questions whenever a friend or co-worker came back from a vacation or weekend trip. Where did they stay? What did they do? How much did they spend? I was particularly interested in people who liked to go on weekend get-a-ways to locations within driving distance. I filed all the details.

I also wanted accommodations that either had a small kitchen or at least a refrigerator and microwave. That way, I could bring my own breakfast and eat out for one large meal, allowing me to take leftovers and reheat them, making another meal.

I began gathering snacks, nuts, and dried fruit for my retreats so I wouldn't have to shop too much before or during my retreat. These little treats were a nourishing break during a retreat, just a fun little pick-me-up.

As a solo traveler, I wanted my accommodations to be safe. I investigated what looked like a good deal but might not have been in the safest part of town. I asked around, talked to hotel/motel staff, the Airbnb host, and read reviews – I looked at it all.

I made note of the positives in my life:

- I had a dependable and economical car with good gas mileage.

- I had a mortgage and living expenses low enough that I was able to work part-time and take three days off – Friday, Saturday, and Sunday. I could leave Thursday after work and return late on Sunday, giving me three full days of writing-retreat bliss.

- I had very few family obligations.

- I had limited my volunteer work over the years so I could write on my days off.

- I had limited my friends to those who were supportive of my writing lifestyle.

- I had a supportive partner who understood my need to write without distractions.

As I looked at all this, I realized that I had already carved out a writing life for myself at home. Now, it was just a matter of putting together an out of-the-ordinary writing retreat.

Scheduling

I looked at my calendar and picked out weekends with events that I could either move around or cancel all together. I earmarked and scheduled a three-day writer's retreat each month throughout the year. Just to be safe, I marked an extra weekend if I had an opening, just in case one fell through for a reason that I couldn't foresee. Marking these weekends in bold ink on my calendar anchored them firmly into the physical plane. With this in place, I began to visualize writing retreats as a normal routine for myself.

The first retreat I scheduled, I told friends that I was going on a writer's retreat on an upcoming date and would be unavailable, except for emergencies. My friends were so happy that I had scored a big writer's retreat, as if I had been selected for one of the expensive paid writer's symposiums. I let them think this for the first couple of retreats, until they caught on that I was going on my own private writer's retreats. Because of their initial admiration of a coveted writer's retreat at first, it trained them not to call or whine about me being out of town and unavailable.

Before I went on my first out-of-town writer's retreat, though, it was important for me to start small with valuable in-town ones. This allowed me to get a feel for what I would need and want to make my longer retreats comfortable and successful.

Start with Small Retreats

If you have never had a private writer's retreat, it's a good idea to start with a small one. Schedule a few hours during the week to go somewhere locally to write. It is important to get out of the house and have trial runs. These hourly writer's retreats give us practice and information about what we may need for future and longer retreats.

Mini retreats promote confidence and a feeling of what it might be like to have extended time away. Plus, it gives us the immediate writer's retreat that we crave so badly. We can easily schedule several hourly writer's retreats in town into our weekdays or weekends to give us quicker access to wonderful, productive writing time.

In order to start with smaller retreats, look around in your daily wanderings for new places to write. An ideal private writing space could be by local water resources – a river, beach, lake, or sitting on the dock of the bay.

Go to resorts and hotels in your area for a morning or afternoon. You do not have to pay for a room to sit by the fireplace in the lobby or on the grounds of a hotel or resort. I have even found empty conference rooms or small executive meeting spaces with comfortable chairs, tables, and fabulous views.

Look for benches and seating areas that have electricity close by. If there is a light or a sign, there is usually an outlet. Resorts are service-oriented, and it is a possibility that you could purchase and be served a drink or meal, depending on where you are sitting.

One year, I was needing to rehearse a Power Point presentation with my new high-tech projector and remote. I went on a Saturday to a resort close by that hosts many conferences. As I walked in the door, I saw there was, indeed, a conference going on and went to look for an small empty room, as the attendees were all gathered in the main ballroom.

I was wandering about and saw a suitable room that would be ideal for me to rehearse in. A hotel worker approached me and asked if he could be of service. I told him I needed to rehearse for a later presentation with my new equipment and asked if the room I had picked would be okay to use. He said he would check.

He went through the service doors in the hall and came back and said that the room was open until 1 pm. It was 10 a.m. at the time. I told him I didn't need to move anything other than to set up my equipment and rehearse. He wanted to help me, but I told him I needed to know all the details of my equipment and how long it would take me to set up, so I would have an idea of how early I needed to be at the event. He nodded and said that if I needed anything further, to let him know. I thanked him and closed the door.

I had a full two-hour rehearsal of my presentation that day and knew exactly how much time I needed to set up. Power Points and projectors have a mind of their own sometimes, and I needed to learn the ins and outs of this new equipment. That rehearsal allowed me to make my mistakes and push all the wrong buttons prior, so my future presentation was as organized and professional as possible.

Later that week, my presentation went off without a hitch. I was right on time with prep because of this ability to rehearse at the resort.

Museums have free days and offer quiet nooks and sometimes eating areas surrounded by art. Libraries have meeting and study rooms. Parks have picnic tables. Hospitals have chapels. Bookstores have reading chairs. Buildings have court yards. College campuses are the best for writing since they usually have a food court, library, open classrooms, areas outside under trees or patios, and best of all, public bathrooms.

I was on the University of Arizona campus recently, and on the lower level of Old Main, I spotted a table with chairs overlooking the gardens and fountain. I said to my companion, "This would be where I would study if I was a student." Then it dawned on me, I could use it now as a place to write! Even though I am actively looking for and having writing retreats often, I still sometimes have a near miss in noticing an ideal location for a small writing retreat.

It is important to file these writing spots away so when you want to go write locally, your choices will be at your fingertips. Write a note of which are good for outdoor writing and those that have indoor areas, so you have choices no matter what the weather, season, or time of day for your writing retreat. Note which have electricity, Wi-Fi, comfy chairs, good views, and close parking. I recommend taking a photo so when life once again gets hectic, you have a visual of your small writer's retreat location. Pictures speak volumes; allow that image to remind you of the freedom and joy you felt writing there as well.

If you look, you will be amazed at all the options available for ideal writing in your own city or town. The suburbs, developments, and retirement communities often have community centers and trails lined with benches throughout their property. Many hotels will also offer staycations during the off season with phenomenal deals. Research, pay attention, and stay aware to possible writing locations and you will be amazed at how many ideal places there are, even in the smallest of towns.

Research How Other Writers Retreat

Read about writers and how they get away to write for inspiration. J.K. Rowling, the author of the Harry Potter books, wrote daily in Edinburgh, Scotland, at local cafés. She said in an interview that cafés were the best place for her to write, and she liked that she didn't have to make her own coffee. She would get out of the house and write where she was warm and not distracted by her daily life. She liked cafés that weren't too crowded but had enough customers so she could "blend in." They were also ideal for her because when she got stuck on a thought or needed to take a break, she would just walk to another café, sit down, and begin writing again.

J.K. Rowling wasn't wealthy early on, and she made her own daily private writer's retreat that worked for her. She said now that she is famous, she is unable to work anonymously in cafés anymore and checks into luxury suites at hotels for her writing retreats. Nice.

Natalie Goldberg, a prolific author and writing teacher, writes in coffee shops in Taos, New Mexico. She orders a warm drink and something to nibble on, then writes to her heart's desire. It doesn't cost much, and she too gets out of the house and routine to focus on writing.

These writers and so many more have figured out places to write that are close to home, but not home, all within a short drive or walking distance. This is considered a writing retreat, as well – you retreat to write. When we expand our thoughts about what a writing retreat is, we open to greater and new possibilities and productivity.

Personally, I love airline flights, being strapped in for those few precious hours 35,000 feet in the air to write, write, write. The flight attendant delivers a snack with drink and I only get up to take a bathroom break. Nirvana! But now I have many more options than those glorious hours in the sky.

If you are a commuter and use a subway, bus, or train to get to work, utilize this time to be productive as a moving writer's retreat, if you will. You won't regret the time spent whizzing through the city or countryside writing.

Many a book and screenplay was written while the author was on their break or lunch hour. Look for private times that you can transform for profitable use.

Simple Tools

We are so lucky to have writing as our creative outlet. An artist is usually stuck in the studio, composers may need to be close to a piano or sound studio, a ceramicist stays close to their clay table and kiln. But we, as writers, need only the basic tools of pen and paper to create. We are very portable. We can write virtually anywhere.

Most of us use laptop computers. We can go throughout the world and plug in or have an extra battery pack in tow. But that equipment isn't essential in order to write. I have used napkins at restaurants, a program at a concert, the back of my hand, and if all else fails, toilet paper.

One can easily go to a secluded place called the bathroom and write on an unlimited amount of toilet paper and paper towels. Paper is everywhere in there. I then stuff what I have written in my purse or pocket for later and no one is the wiser. That way, I do not lose ideas or dialogue anywhere. I always carry a pen wherever I go for these impromptu writing retreats. They can pop up in the most interesting places.

During the pandemic, we were encouraged to stay at home. We had to socially distance which was an unexpected opportunity to write. But again, at home distractions were great with increased family time, TV news, Zoom, preparation for the isolation, home projects, etc. It was tough and scary to get out of the house with mask in hand and go on a writer's retreat. However, our vehicles made for climate-controlled, comfortable isolation pods. During isolation, it was even more vital to have an out-of-the-house writer's retreat. We could park anywhere with a view and write safely.

Many of us used our stay-at-home restrictions to reevaluate and reclaim a writing room or space with thicker boundaries to isolate ourselves from distractions. However, we all probably found that nothing was better than getting in the car and getting out of there for a change of scenery. Cars and trucks became Retreat Vehicles – RVs, if you must.

As you look for and utilize local writing-retreat options, start to visualize longer periods of time and out-of-town retreats for the future. Remember, these hourly writing times are vital for now *and* later.

Longer Writer's Retreats

The basic premise for a writing retreat is <u>undisturbed</u> time to write. It is a container for writing bordered by time, space, and you. A longer retreat creates a stretch of days allowing your writer's lifestyle to emerge uninterrupted. It is the ability to immerse in an aura you deem important to you as a writer.

Writer's retreats ignite the spark for creativity to happen. This means a span of time to ponder and be open to new ideas. It is also your chance to read those books and magazines, peruse the internet, take a marketing course on YouTube, or anything that will inspire and guide you to new avenues with your writing. It gives precious seclusion for inspiration to catch up and flood over us.

To write sixteen hours straight can be done, and I am sure there are writers who do just that, but a writer's retreat can also have a slowness, a release from pressure, a more relaxed atmosphere to find your own writing rhythm. If we are stuffing our writing within our already busy lives, there is a heaviness of burden to use those small, precious portions of time to write. But on an extended writer's retreat, we can ease up a bit, find what works for us and actually live a full-time writing lifestyle for the period we have allowed.

A writer's retreat is for writer's self-care as well. It isn't just about writing for hours upon hours, unless you want or need to get a project done. Instead, it encourages a comfortable writing pace to show itself. The inner writer will begin to have a noticeable voice again. To be with oneself, to listen, converse, and journal is cleansing and oh, so necessary.

Writing retreats are filled with intuitive guidance, pointing to the next step in our writing. We allow the flow to carry us for the duration of the retreat. We may get an insight to write in a different genre, try something new, take a risk, get up in the middle of the night, or stay up writing 'til dawn. We can do whatever we are led to do, to have fun and explore, to study and relax.

There is comfort knowing that this will not be the only writer's retreat you will have this year. Relax into it and know there is an abundance and no lack of anything on your retreat.

You may go to a town that is or resembles the setting of your book or play. You may need to go to the museum or library for research or to put yourself in an exact location to be surrounded by atmosphere and dialogue.

We tend to listen more intently to those around us when we are alone, hearing the nuances of speech and breathe in the richness of a culture. All is up to us and what we need for our writing. Retreating is a ticket to whatever adventures we want and need to continue our work.

One retreat, I was at an abbey in Arizona with the door open on a lovely spring morning, over-looking the fields of gently swaying lush grasses. The birds were singing, all was well. I was reading my latest short story out loud as I revised it. Later, I found out at lunch, that this was a *silent* abbey for *silent* retreaters. Oops! From then on, I respected the silence. Luckily, there were very few residing in the rooms close to where I was at.

I liked the silent retreat house; no one talked in the kitchen or while eating at the table. It had a stocked spiritual library with a soft, overstuffed chair and good lighting. It was ideal. I learned to appreciate the contemplative culture of the retreat and wrote articles about the value of silence in our world. I breathed in this monastic breath while there. It was a valuable writing retreat that had deeper levels of inspiration, along with an abundance of writing productivity.

For me, to submerge in these writing marathons for a few days is heaven on Earth. I never know what will come out of a writer's retreat. If I stay open and flexible to the environment, more than expected will be my reward.

Who Goes with You on Writer's Retreat?

No one! This is not a vacation – it is a working, tax-deductible time away from distractions. No animals, no children, no adults, no family, no friends. It is not a time to schedule a visit with a nearby relative one night for dinner; it will take valuable time away from writing as you dress for, drive to, and eat this dinner. It is your precious time to write that you have just given to someone else.

Stick to yourself and your writing; you might have had the best writing of your life during those very hours you spent visiting a friend or relative. You and I have to draw the line. You don't have to tell the relative or friend you are on a writing retreat in their area, just keep it to yourself and protect this private space.

If you have trouble traveling alone pretend you live in the town you are retreating in. At home we go to the store alone, get gas for the car alone, shop alone – why be so worried about going alone to the store or anywhere else in a new town? Look around, people are doing their errands by themselves there too.

Relax and enjoy your new hometown for the time you are there. You have the freedom to go and do anything you want to do, wherever you are. Explore a bit of your new writing retreat locale. You will find ideal writing spaces there just as easily as at home. Chances are, you will be returning for future retreats. Be friendly to the service providers as if you live there. They may know of a great restaurant that wouldn't otherwise be known.

Some people do not like to eat out alone. Researching online restaurants and menus is a must. We can call and order takeout. Once you pick food up, go to a park, the courtyard of where you are staying, or back to your room. Fast food is readily available and grocery stores usually have single portions or delis. Go on a picnic.

One of my favorite towns for writing retreat is Sedona which has a large natural market, and I usually eat my deli sandwich or salad on one of their famous vortexes. It is free and accessible to go to these amazing sacred sites. Feel the energy, take in the view, and after lunch, sit and write with Mother Nature. Nurture the soul while nourishing the body.

Another favorite writing retreat location of mine is a small-town Airbnb that has a local Mexican restaurant right across the street. I order by phone or bring reading material to the restaurant and order take out. Then I cross the street to my casita and eat on the patio, watching hummingbirds flitting from blossom to blossom next to my table.

You may think I spend a fortune at these prime locations, but I don't. I have found through internet research and asking folks about their favorite places to stay, many affordable accommodations.

Writing at luxury hotels and resorts doesn't mean you have to afford to rent a room from them. For example, I went on a writing retreat in Douglas, Arizona. Douglas is a border town in the southeast corner of the state. I found a cheap motel with rave reviews. I think I paid $39 a night. It was a clean, family-owned motel. There was even a popular breakfast café next door.

Each morning, I would take my laptop to the grand, historic Gadsden Hotel in the middle of this quaint town. On the second floor, I discovered a large, covered balcony area with tables and cushioned chairs. It was so comfortable that I spent most of my writing retreat at that second-floor oasis. Amazingly, few people came into the secluded area. Once in a while, tourists would open the door, look over the edge of the balcony to the street below, and move on quietly.

Since the Gadsden Hotel is in town, I could hear a bit of traffic noise below, but it wasn't disturbing. When night came, I was happy to go back to my little motel in the quieter residential area to sleep and didn't have the nightly $250+ price tag for a room.

Where to Go Within A Budget

Go ahead, check out the paid writing retreats. They are great, and even though they cost money and have an application process, they sometimes offer scholarships or grants. Some are affordable on even the tightest budget.

Universities, colleges, and libraries usually have "writer in residence" programs. They want a writer to offer office hours and give lectures/presentations/workshops to students or the community. These opportunities usually come with an office space, access to loads of resources and faculty, and can be springboards for your writing career.

Keep researching and submitting applications. You never know what writing retreat options will open up. One good retreat option will always lead to another. There is usually a long process between application, acceptance, and the beginning of these programs, so in the meantime, go on your own private writing retreats. Sprinkle your months with all opportunities that refresh and inform your writing.

Obviously, the most convenient private writing retreat spaces are hotels, motels, private cottages, mountain cabins, Airbnbs, RVs, tiny houses, she/he sheds, campgrounds, state and national parks, the desert, beach, or in the woods. Find what fits into your spending plan, do not let money be the deterrent for writing peace.

Mountains and hills have rocks to sit on all over their slopes. A forest-ranger friend of mine told me about a famous poet who had a favorite rock she sat on close to the ranger station. Apparently, she wrote many poetry books sitting on that rock.

Louis L'Amour, the legendary western writer, would go to the little mountain town of Durango, Colorado, with his family for the month of August each year for over ten years. He would rent rooms at The Strater Hotel. His private writing room was the corner room above the Diamond Belle Saloon. He would hike those majestic mountains with the family after his writing hours were over. The staff were gracious and honored by his presence and accommodated his privacy and his family's recreational needs.

If you don't want to hike in, campgrounds and benches abound. There is a popular bench under a tree on a trail near the base of Bell Rock in Oak Creek Village, Arizona. People are usually respectful when they see someone writing, drawing, painting, or playing music and will pass by without a word. I have found affordable lodging nearby in the Village. Years ago, I was writing for weeks at a time there when working on one of my books.

I booked a suite at a lodge at an affordable rate on the second floor. During the week, the rates were better than reasonable, and I would return home on the busy and noisy weekend. It was at a time when I had accumulated many hours of paid time off at my employment. I saved as many hours as possible those years solely for longer writing retreats.

This suite had a bedroom, kitchenette, and view of towering red rock formations. I would walk around the back streets on breaks and frequent the same restaurants so much that they got to know me. It was home away from home for that period of time. The point is, be friendly and at home wherever you go. These are your new-hometown neighbors.

Before booking a room, ask yourself if this is a safe, clean, climate-controlled space to write. It's hard to concentrate when you are freezing and your fingers are numb, or too hot and sweat drips onto your papers and computer. If you are looking at outdoor writing retreats, get a weather app on your phone and look for the days that are the perfect temperature, no wind, rain or snow. Be particular with this because a windy day can blow your papers and thoughts into the next county. It can be distracting running to retrieve your newest chapters.

For overnight retreats, look for a suitable bed, table, chair, good lighting, refrigerator, and microwave. Ask lots of questions before booking if you can. Mostly be honest with yourself. This isn't a time to go into survival mode; it is important to be comfortable during your writing retreat. If you do not like the place you are staying at, once you are in that town, you can look for better accommodations and move if you wish.

Most accommodations have basic electricity and Wi-Fi. But just in case, I now have a small, folding solar panel that is light and packable. It lies out in the sun next to me and charges my computer, devices, and phone. I can stop at any time off road to write for a day and still be plugged in.

My portable-hotspot Wi-Fi device has been a miracle worker for me. It is secured and, oh, so handy when I need it most. I will often use my own Wi-Fi instead of the public or hotel's for added security and avoid the hassle of finding the password or paying a fee. Now, I can have Wi-Fi anywhere there is phone service. It is worth the small monthly fee I pay, and it is smaller than my phone.

At times you may need large blank walls to tape pages of your book, article, or story boards on. This is an easy way to organize ideas and move them around. You can move chapters, scenes, and characters around easily. Sleeping with ideas and chapters surrounding you is ideal, for in the morning, it may offer a new perspective that can be shifted quickly into a new place on the wall.

As I live with my stories and characters around me in this way, much can happen that would normally have to be "put off" at home or in the office. The delay of writing down an idea or dialogue can cause it to fade and be forgotten into eternity. Having the story on walls with a marker close by allows me to catch that idea immediately and put it in its proper place with ease.

I find that it is easier to move pages, sentences, plot points, characters, ideas or whatever around on the wall rather than on a computer at first. Once I have it all in place where I want it, then it can be moved securely onto my computer again. First drafts are always a bit messy, but being surrounded by the whole book on four walls to view and live in, gives a heightened overview and sense of flow.

In Florida, I used to offer mansion-sitting services. These were large, beautiful homes where the owners wanted someone to live on their estates while they traveled, usually abroad. Having a person on the property offered security, as it seemed as if the owners were at home and not on an extended vacation. Perfect writing retreat.

One mansion had a large outside pool, and in the evenings, I would swim watching the evening stars and moon phases. I found my opportune writing room in that house overlooking the manicured gardens and tall hedges. When I needed to change locations, though, I would write in a different part of the house or yard. I wrote in the sunroom, the garden, the parlor, the library, by the water fountain, and under the swaying palms. Yes, I did write out in the cabana as well.

House sitting for friends is ideal too, and word spreads that you are available for hire to stay in someone's house when they are away. These are house sitting and not pet sitting jobs. This is important as those cuddly, cute pets are very distracting and come with a greater responsibility than I want for writer's retreat. I also make sure the houses and mansions are spotless and back to original placement of items when I leave.

Housesitting in large cities has its advantages due to the large number of resources available, but I am in favor of staying in smaller towns. In a small town I can get to know a few people and it is easier to get around. If I go to a large city to mansion sit, I do not stray far from where I am staying but focus my life within a few blocks if possible. I don't sightsee unless it is part of my retreat goals – I go to write.

Dealing with Excuses & Reasons Not to Go

Once you have scheduled your trip and secured your room, there may come a time when fear creeps up. You may want to talk yourself out of the retreat. This is normal. Here are some of my writer's retreat sabotage thoughts:

"It is too expensive for me to go. I could use that money and time for something else."

"I don't know anyone."

"My car might break down, or I could have a heart attack (or break a leg, hurt my back) and there wouldn't be anyone around to help."

"I will miss my family, dog, cat, routine…"

"I should stay at home and do the yardwork, paint the kitchen, or clean out the garage."

Every out-of-town writer's retreat I go on, there is usually a period when my thoughts are trying to talk me out of it. And I go on writer's retreats often. I don't know what it is that scares me. It could be being alone in a strange place or looking at this time as a blank page, unsure what I am going to put on it.

I don't know what to look forward to other than time to write, which is usually motivation enough. Having this clean slate gives me a canvas to create something amazing. So, it is with a writer's retreat.

We don't know what it will be like or what masterpieces we will come up with until we actually go and do it. Excuses and reasons not to go will pop up. Say to yourself, "I am all ready to go. I have been waiting for this opportunity to have a writer's retreat for a long time. It is a dream. I need to just get in the car (or on the flight) and see what happens. I can always leave whenever I want during the retreat, and never do it again if it doesn't work for me. I'll go this once and see if I like it or get writing done." Work through this negative thinking and Just Do It!

I have the most productive times on writer's retreats. I have gotten unstuck on a problem piece or area in my writing. I have jumped into new territory, spent needed time on marketing, and had new ideas that I allowed to flow undisturbed. Writing retreats have given me new enthusiasm, and I have been refreshed in my writing like nothing else in my life.

Let the universe guide you. You are ready to go, now just get in the car!

What to Bring

If we drive to our private writing retreat location, we can bring more with us than in a suitcase for a flight. It is easy to pack essentials for us writers; like I said, we really only need paper and something to write with. However, we can take books, a folding chair, printer, camera, paper, a laptop, Wi-Fi, our phone, food/snacks, water, a beach towel, portable umbrella, suitable comfortable clothing, drinks, medications, headphones, a swimsuit, hiking boots, toiletries, and projects. Whatever you would take when going on a trip for as long as you plan to go.

One of the most important items I take is what I call my rolling office. I bought a wheeled computer/carry-on from an office supply store several years ago. It has tons of compartments inside and expands as space is needed.

My rolling office has gone with me all over this country. It has been perfect for presentations, signings, workshops, and writing retreats. It is so much better than a backpack, over-the-shoulder bag, or computer case. This small piece of luggage has three larger compartments and loads of medium and small pockets, some with Velcro. It is big enough to hold: a small printer, paper, a laptop, electronic devices, a hot spot, a projector, all my pens, flash drives, scotch tape, highlighters, chargers, extra power cords, protein bars, a water bottle, sticky notes, business cards, headphones, magazines, marketing materials, books, my purse, and a lunch.

I have even stuck another large bag on top of it and raced through airports, no problem. Even though it sounds like there is a lot in there, I can easily lift it into an overhead compartment or place it under the seat on a plane. It also rolls down the thin airplane aisle quickly. I only wish it came with a motor and a seat for me to ride.

I take it on my in-town writing retreats as well. I don't have to think about what to pack, for over the years, everything I need is in there. When I get low on supplies, I make a note and the next time I am at a store or on Amazon, I buy it and put it directly into my rolling office upon delivery. Keeping my rolling office stocked is first priority.

Event organizers have been panicked when they realize they don't have that extra extension cord for my equipment and gratefully amazed when I pull one out of my bag. My rolling office is highly organized; everything has its place. Before I leave an event or retreat, I quickly inventory to make sure I have everything I brought with me and all is packed away tight.

I throw my rolling office into my trunk whenever I go out of the house now. Once, I forgot and had to lug too much stuff and regretted that I didn't have what I needed. As we become more portable writers, we never know where we might end up once we leave the house. Don't miss an unexpected hour or two for a quick and equipped writer's retreat.

Before I go on an extended writer's retreat, I print out and check off a generic list of commonly used items. Things that I will need that I may forget like a hair dryer, portable iron, hangers, and such. I do have a cosmetic case that has travel-size lotions, shampoos, sunscreen, deodorants, etc. that I also keep stocked. When I return from a writer's retreat, I refill all my smaller tubes and bottles. That way I can go on a moment's notice and be on the road within a half hour if I want.

I also make a list of goals before a retreat, just to remember to bring materials for certain projects. Even though I have a "To Do" list, I don't allow it to stifle my flexibility or pressure me, which can cause me to block while on retreat. I always leave space for inspiration, intuition, and the unexpected to augment my writer's retreat.

On one writer's retreat at an Airbnb, the host had several books on the table, and one was about flash fiction. I started to read it and couldn't set it down. Afterwards, I had a great conversation with the host who was also a writer. He told me that the Fat Tire bikes that he provided for guests were a prize he won at a flash-fiction contest from the Fat Tire Beer company. I enjoyed riding that Fat Tire Beer bike throughout town on break. This writer's retreat also greatly inspired my "flash" writing.

As I allow for flexibility with my "To Do" list, I also make a "Done" or "Did" list on a writer's retreat. I write everything I have accomplished throughout the day, even the most mundane. This gives me a sense of completion, accomplishment, and productivity, even if I went off track from what my original expectations were. I have many writer's retreats, so I know I can catch up on other goals later. The unforeseen opportunities that an out-of-town retreat offers are not to be missed. Stay open to where your muse leads you.

I also bring magazines that I want to query, inspiring books, or other materials that I want to read and haven't had the time. Anything that will enlighten me is important on a writer's retreat. Some books I peruse, others I read cover to cover. I may leave books and magazines, when finished, at the place I am staying.

Since I usually have several projects I am working on at one time, I bring them all in their various stages. If I come to a stopping place on one piece, I can pick up another with fresh eyes. They may be new ideas I want to explore, first drafts, revisions, or final proofs. I find I work better with multiple avenues open instead of working only on one project at a time. It just works for me but may not for everyone.

I also like to read the local newspaper wherever I am. Who has time for that anymore? Small-town papers are fun to read, and they have information about events and allow you to immerse in the local culture. There can be information about bookstores and points of interest that you would not normally be aware of.

One time, I went to the annual town picnic/barbeque at the local park that I had seen advertised in their weekly paper. It was a fun way to have dinner out with a large group of friendly people. The local businesses and organizations had tables set up with giveaway items.

I picked up objects that I used on my retreat: a water bottle, pens and pads of paper(!), a letter opener, sticky notes, snacks, sunscreen, lip balm, cozies, neon markers, bubbles, and a little flashlight key chain, all in a fabric bag with the town's name on it. I got to sit in the local firetruck and had my photo taken. I have grand memories of that writer's retreat, and I still fondly use my free gifts to this day.

Pack whatever you need to have a comfortable, safe, and productive writer's retreat. Take writing and reading material you want to focus on because, usually, sometime during your reclusiveness, you will become bored and want to distract. If you have plenty of projects available, you can refocus to the next writing or reading task at hand.

What Not To Do

No media unless it is related to your work. No TV, Netflix, Hulu, Disney+, Amazon Prime, Alexa, Social Media, Facebook, Twitter, Google, TikTok, Instagram, or Video Games, etc., unless you use these for marketing, inspiration, or writing focus. If social media is part of what you need to be doing during your writing retreat, i.e., marketing, researching genres, reading an inspirational book, Skyping, or a Zoom conference with your agent, illustrator, publicist, editor, publisher or…then do it. But for entertainment purposes, these exclusive moments are all about your writing career – don't be tempted.

It is important to limit distractions and not bring items that will seduce you away from your writing intention. Instead, entertain yourself with your own humor, crazy stories or making up a screenplay of what you would like to watch on that TV staring at you. Make writing retreat productive and fun. You will be surprised at what you can create. Be wild with your writing!

Remember, you can have a mini retreat at any time, even during your longer retreats. Go to a nearby museum, art gallery, or historical site. Take your computer or journal with you, for these are inspiring places to write and birth new ideas.

I was staying in an Airbnb and had worked very hard all morning. I needed a change of scenery. A couple of miles from where I was staying was a historic abandoned mission protected by the National Parks Service. I paid a modest entrance fee, looked at my map, and as I turned a corner, I came upon a bench against an ancient adobe wall looking out through an arched patio with a perfect view of this majestic southwest mission. The adobe mission was breathtaking. It stood proud in the desert sun with towering mountains in the background. I immediately sat down and took out my laptop. I was so glad I had left my accommodations and found this perfect place to write.

Occasionally, a guided tour group would walk past. After taking photos and hearing the story, they would move on to the next photo op, moving swiftly like a covey of quail. My discovery of this mission was the highlight of that writer's retreat. Writing in the shade on these ancient sacred grounds that glorious spring day will always be in my memory. I took photos and walked the paths when I needed a break. I wrote prolifically until they closed at dusk.

If I had turned on the TV or checked my social media instead of exploring the area I was in, I would have missed this mission and hours of inspired writing. Social media can be a time killer and I need to keep boundaries on my precious writing retreats. I was able to have a smaller writer's retreat within my larger one by simply changing writing locations.

Once You Arrive

I try to arrive before night falls and check into my accommodations quickly. This way I have time to unpack and take a small tour of the area. This not only helps me know where I am in town, but also what is available close by. I orient myself by saying, "This is my new home. Let's see what adventures are possible here."

Make home wherever you are. Home is where we are – we are always at home inside, not out. Make the best of what the area has to offer, but remember you are there for writer's retreat, so again, try to locate optimal writing places as you tour.

Be friendly and get acquainted with the staff and service providers; they are your new friends while you are visiting. They have much information and are there to assist. You will always have someone to go to if the need arises, and it will help you feel more secure wherever you land.

I usually ask housekeeping not to come for a few days, so I am not disturbed. But I do ask for extra towels and toilet paper. If I am there for longer than a couple of days, I leave when they clean the room, vacuum, and change linens. I may let the staff know that I am a writer and need privacy to do my work. They always accommodate my needs and know that I will be a nice, quiet guest.

One writer's retreat was in a hot and dusty mining community. It was close to a state park that offered free hot springs – thank you, Universe. But I stayed mostly in my motel room on a small highway in town, as it turned cold and rained much of the few days I was there. I was very productive on that retreat, as I stayed in my room except for my noon meal as I ate leftovers heated by the microwave for dinner. I brought plenty of food with me to fill the small refrigerator and was sequestered comfortably.

After dinner, I could hear men who were staying at the motel talking in the parking lot.

They were contractors who seemed to congregate by their company trucks to talk amongst themselves. They were harmless and weren't very loud. When they went to their rooms to sleep, that was when I stopped too and enjoyed a quiet slumber.

The next day, we were all up at the crack of dawn, me working on my computer and them leaving for their work around the area. I felt like a stealth comrade to them. They didn't know I existed, but they became a constant hum for me when they returned each night.

That cozy old motel was ideal for me, even though it was not where I would vacation. It had a sturdy table and chair, microwave, refrigerator, comfy bed with nice linens, clean bathroom, sweet staff, and good lighting. It also had plenty of electrical outlets and a recliner for reading. I just tucked in on those rainy days and wrote, wrote, wrote.

Usually, After a Couple of Days, Negative Self-Talk Begins Again

On most writer's retreats, after a few days in, I can get bored, lonely, or just over it. I start talking myself into going home. The novelty has worn off and I have usually worked very hard. I plan for this doubt and these lonesome thoughts to happen and have come to realize that this is a vital pivotal point during each writer's retreat.

After about an hour into my negative self-talk, something shifts in my writing. I actually get better clarity, work through a block, and the magic of the writer's retreat happens with my writing. After these small bouts of wanting to go home or see what my peeps are doing, my writing begins to loosen. I do some of my most honest writing after this point. Stick it out and you will be rewarded.

At first, I didn't know that would be the case and thought long and hard about leaving early. If I do something different such as go for a walk, get something to eat, take a nap, drive to another writing location in the area or write about my feelings and thoughts, it relieves my restlessness.

Do not panic and begin to pack. If you allow yourself to have these thoughts, let them drift by like a cloud overhead, it will pass. Remember what a gift you are giving yourself by being there; a dream come true.

Every time – EVERY TIME – I walk through this time of wanting to leave, the good stuff happens. I recommit to staying and I always break through and have fun with writing. I have even allowed myself to write something totally different – what the heck. Since there is nothing distracting that I will allow myself to do to get out of this, I will either tackle a block or hard task, but mostly, I will catapult into some sort of refreshing writing. Writing can change from then on into a different level of creativity.

The Plan and No Plan

Writer's retreats can start with a plan, but it is imperative to allow the flow and journey of the retreat energy to happen. A plan is a direction we wish to go, but it needs to be flexible and may even be discarded completely as we follow the flow of each writing day. A side trip or two may catch our interest and set us on a completely new path. It is important to our sanity and creativity to be malleable enough to try not to will ourselves to follow "The Plan" but to stay open to explore and follow the opportunities presented.

As I talked earlier, I had a plan, when I went to the abbey, to finish a project, but switched to writing about the power of silence and contemplation. This better plan unexpectedly presented itself. This happens often on writer's retreats, unless I really do have a strict deadline. Even if I do, there is always an allowance to follow a scent on the wind if I want. If I do, I inevitably find that I finish my project and complete another piece that was unexpected and a joy.

Does this give me too much looseness that I get lost in sloth? No, it gives me the ability to follow whatever is catching my attention in the moment and day. Go where the open door is instead of always beating down with self-will that which is blocked and barred. It is exhausting to try to bully our way through a writing piece. Amazingly, the willingness to follow the spirit of each particular writing retreat will lead to productive, varied, and fresh writing.

Ending the Writer's Retreat

Now, it really is time to go back home. You have done it. Even if you are in the middle of a project, you now have a good, solid direction for your next steps. The good news is, there are other writer's retreats already on your calendar.

We gather, organize, and pack up; having eaten the food, streamlined our work, and rested, we are lighter for the return trip, inside and out. Leaving writing retreats may come with a sense of longing for it to continue, accomplishment for working hard, and having a different perspective on our writing. There is also an excitement to return to our familiar routine at home and talk about our adventures.

We now have experience and have learned what we could do differently or better with each retreat we go on. Look at your "Done" list and all you accomplished. Reflect on how important it was and now you can return refreshed and your writing tank is full again. Plan for your next long writer's retreat and know this isn't just a once-in-a-lifetime happening. You have the ability to plan and go on writer's retreats often. You will be energized with what you have gained on this writer's retreat, and that will spill over into your week and sometimes even last until your next get-a-way.

If I get stuck in between writer's retreats, I know there is a good possibility I will unstick on my next retreat. There is less worry if my work is paused for a while, as trust develops that there is a way through soon with intentional private time and space.

Each writing retreat is unique and has its own enchantment. If you took photos while on retreat for inspiration and memories, these images can be used on websites, books, or hanging around the house or over our desks. They are reminders of the energy and what we gained from each of these excursions.

Think about where you may want to go next. Maybe an update of accommodations, a state park, in an RV, or camping in the mountains. It is all up to you now; you have freedom to write wherever you want. Have fun picking your next location and go somewhere you have never been but want to visit. Writing is our ticket to the world – punch that ticket often.

Kermie Wohlenhaus

Unexpected Writer's Retreats

Sometimes, the universe will open up unexpected time for us. For example, a friend called the other day and said that she was upset because her PRN job hadn't called her to work for a few days now. She was in the midst of writing her dissertation and was worried about money. She mumbled through tears that she probably needed to look into downsizing her apartment, find a more stable position, get married to a rich person, worried, worried, worried.

I said, "You have the gift of an unexpected writer's retreat! This is your opportunity to write on your dissertation; don't blow it by worrying, getting upset, or distracting yourself with fear. GO WRITE! Be grateful for the time off. You have the money saved in case you were called off from all your holiday work. Take it!"

She thanked me later, as she did take my suggestion. She said she got a tremendous amount of writing and research done on her dissertation during those weeks when work was slow. As she continued to use her down time for writing, she graduated with her Ph.D. sooner than expected. She was so glad to have harnessed the energy of her emotions to work for her, which gave her a deep and productive focus. She didn't have to change a thing in her life except to utilize this down time for writing, which eventually did change her life circumstances.

It was a reminder for me also. I've had unexpected days off many times. I take stock of my finances and note that I am still solvent and prepared financially for such days and weeks, then look up to the Universe and say, "Thank you, for now I have an unexpected writer's retreat!"

Name your unexpected delays and unplanned time off as mini writer's retreats. Use the down time in the waiting area at the tire store, dentist office, or anywhere you have to sit and wait. These are unexpected gifts. It will change frustration into the most productive writing time you may have that week.

The shift to be aware and utilize this extra time can be vital to us writers. Do not waste it with distractions and worry but turn it into moments of creativity. You are a writer and will thank yourself for being able to have mini writing retreats anywhere you can take them. The universe is working with you to co-create these undisturbed openings to write. Be grateful for them and then write, Write, WRITE!

Last Words

Take the time and make the effort to have a small writing retreat today and plan an extended one as soon as you can. It will lift your heart and mind knowing that you are carving out time for and honoring your passion and talent. Remember, a writing retreat is as easy as taking a few hours in your day, a few days in your month, or a few months in your year to create an extraordinary writing event.

A writer's retreat is a gift we give ourselves. It is a valuable present waiting to be opened, chock-full of surprises, dilemmas, and adventures. Go ahead, try it and see what treasures you find as you set sail for distant shores to write. It is well worth the effort, as you will see.

We only limit ourselves by not putting pen to paper or fingers on the keys. So, the last words are what my muse always tells me, and I leave them with you – Have Fun & Go Write!

Creating a Solo Writer's Retreat

About the Author

Kermie Wohlenhaus, Ph.D. is an author, angelologist, zinester, and clairvoyant. She has authored the award-winning *Shopping with the Virgin Mary*, *How to Talk and Actually Listen to Your Guardian Angel*, *Mary's Simple Graces* and edited/annotated the foundation series for the field of Angelology including: *The Complete Reference to Angels in the Bible*, *The Quick Reference to Angels in the Bible*, *The Complete Reference to Angels in The Koran (Qur'an)*, and *The Complete Reference to Angels in The Book of Mormon*.

Kermie's Zines include: *Desert Rain*, *Our Day Off*, *Fairy Patch*, *Mary Magdalene Ain't No Ho*, *I Know You Love Me*, *Jesus was a Nice Jewish Boy*, *The Nurses Stood Strong – COVID-19*, *Listening to Our Angels*, *Jesus Loved John*, *Writing Retreat*, and *What Would You Do if a Spaceship Landed in Your Back Yard*. For further information:
www.KermieWohlenhaus.com